funky knitting

TRACY MARSH PUBLICATIONS

about this book

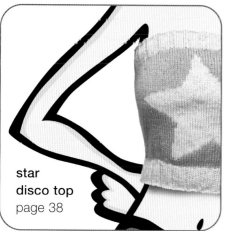

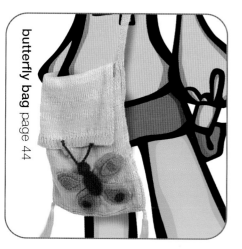

how to
knit
info

about this book

Hey friends,

You are about to have some fab fun knitting up these masterpieces!
Let your imagination go wild, follow these designs and personalise them to suit you or your best buddy.

Now lets get started

1 Choose your favourite project and the correct size.
2 Grab all the materials you will need.
3 Look at the instructions and circle the numbers of your size.
4 If knitting is new to you, go to the back of the book and follow the easy instructions.
5 Get some help if you get stuck.

Look out for the star ratings on each project

  heaps easy!

 easy as!

 try this!

lets start knitting

5

heart beanie

easy
as!

Measurements	Girl		Woman	
To Fit Head	**54cm**		56cm	
	21"		22 "	

Materials
Panda Magnum 8 ply (100g balls)

Green	**1**	1	**1**	1
Blue	**1**	1	**1**	1
Purple	**1**	1	**1**	1
Pink	**1**	1	**1**	1
Yellow	**1**	1	**1**	1
Orange	**1**	1	**1**	1
Red	**1**	1	**1**	I

and Panda Woolbale 50 8 ply (50g balls)

Red	**1**	1	**1**	1

One **set** of 3.75mm (US 5) knitting needles or the required size to give correct tension; knitter's needle for sewing in ends.

Tension
This handknit has been designed at a tension of 23 sts and 32 rows to 10cm (4") over stocking st, using 3.75mm (US 5) needles.

create your own beanie by mixing new colours and changing the icon patch

Hat
Using a **set** of 3.75mm (US 5) needles and Orange, cast on **96** (104) sts.
Work **30** (34) rounds rib as given for Ankle Band of Legwarmers.
Knit **8** (10) rounds each of Red, Green, and Blue.
Knit **2** (10) rounds in Purple.

Woman's Size only -
Change to Pink.

Both Sizes - Beg Crown:

1st Round: * K2tog, K10 (11), rep from * to end ... **88** (96) sts.

2nd and Foll Alt Rounds: Knit.

3rd Round: * K2tog, K9 (10), rep from * to end ... **80** (88) sts.

5th Round: * K2tog, K8 (9), rep from * to end ... **72** (80) sts.

Child's Size only - Knit 1 round. Change to Pink.

Both Sizes - Cont dec in this manner until **40** (64) sts rem. Knit 1 round.
Change to Yellow and cont dec in next and foll alt rounds until 8 sts rem.
Break off yarn, draw through rem sts and fasten off securely.

To make up
Make an Orange pompom 6.5cm (3") in diameter and attach to centre of crown. Make a small felted heart (see page 62) and attach using 'Blanket St' (see page 59). Fold up band.

legwarmers

☆
☆

easy
as!

8

Measurements

	Girl	Girl	Woman	Woman
Length (approx)	**59cm**	65cm	**80cm**	80cm
	23"	25"	**31"**	31"
Around Knee	**31cm**	35cm	**39cm**	43cm
	12"	13"	**15"**	17"

Materials
Panda Magnum 8 ply (100g balls)

	Girl	Girl	Woman	Woman
Green	**1**	1	**1**	1
Blue	**1**	1	**1**	1
Purple	**1**	1	**1**	1
Pink	**1**	1	**1**	1
Yellow	**1**	1	**1**	1
Orange	**1**	1	**1**	1
Red	**1**	1	**1**	1

and Panda Woolbale 50 8 ply (50g balls)

	Girl	Girl	Woman	Woman
Red	**1**	1	**1**	1

One **set** of 3.75mm (US 5) knitting needles or the required size to give correct tension; knitter's needle for sewing in ends.

Tension
This handknit has been designed at a tension of 23 sts and 32 rows to 10cm (4") over stocking st, using 3.75mm (US 5) needles.

Seamless Legwarmers (make 2)

Note: *If desired these legwarmers can be knitted on a pair of needles with a seam up the back. An extra stitch will be needed on each end for the seam. Instead of knitting every round, work in stocking st by working alt rows in purl.*

Using a **set** of 3.75mm (US 5) needles and Green, cast on **56** (56-**60**-64) sts.

Beg Ankle Band:
1st Round: * K2, P2, rep from * to end.
Rep 1st round 19 times (20 rounds in all).

Beg Leg:
Knit 18 rounds.

Next Round: K1, inc in next st, knit to last 2 sts, inc in next st, K1 ... **58** (58-**62**-66) sts.
Knit 1 round.
** Change to Blue and knit 4 rounds.

Next Round: K1, inc in next st, knit to last 2 sts, inc in next st, K1 ... **60** (60-**64**-68) sts.
Knit **3** (4-**5**-5) rounds. **
Rep from ** to ** once in each of Purple, Pink, Yellow, Orange, Red and Green ...
72 (72-**76**-80) sts.
Knit **8** (9-**10**-10) rounds in Blue, then **8** (9-**10**-10) rounds in Purple.

Beg Knee:
Using Pink, knit 44 rounds.

Beg Knee Band:
Using Orange, knit 10 rounds.
Work 30 rounds rib as given for Ankle Band.
Cast off **loosely** in rib.

To make up
Sew in ends. Fold bands onto right side. Make 2 felted hearts (see page 62) and attach using 'Blanket St' (see page 59) to knees as illustrated.

striped poncho

easy as!

Measurements

Measurements	A (yr) 6-8	B (yr) 10-12	C 8-10	D 12-14
Finished Measurement:	**72cm**	82cm	**85cm**	95cm
	29"	33"	**34"**	38"
Length:	**43cm**	46cm	**50cm**	50cm
	17"	18"	**20"**	20"

Materials
Cleckheaton Country 8 ply (50g balls)

1st Contrast (C1)	**2**	2	**2**	3
2nd Contrast (C2)	**2**	2	**2**	2
3rd Contrast (C3)	**1**	2	**2**	2
4th Contrast (C4)	**1**	1	**1**	2
5th Contrast (C5)	**1**	1	**1**	2
6th Contrast (C6)	**1**	1	**1**	1
7th Contrast (C7)	**2**	2	**3**	3

One **pair** of 4.00mm (US 6) and a 4.00mm (US 6) **circular** knitting needle or the required size to give correct tension; knitter's needle for darning in ends.

Tension
This poncho has been designed at tension of 22 sts and 30 rows to 10cm (4") over stocking st, using 4.00mm (US 6)needles.

> maybe i'll knit kellys in baby pink and lemon stripes yeah cool pressie!

Poncho (worked in one piece)

Using 4.00mm (US 6) **circular** needle and C1, cast on **332** (376-**376**-420) sts.

Note: *A circular needle is used to accommodate the number of sts. Work backwards and forwards in rows not rounds.*

1st Row (wrong side): Knit.
2nd Row: Purl.
3rd Row: Knit.
4th Row: K**10** (6-**7**-6), * K2tog, K**8** (9 **10** 9), rep from * to last **12** (7-**9**-7) sts, K2tog, knit to end … **300** (342-**345**-382) sts.
Work **17** (19-**20**-20) rows stocking st, beg with a purl row.

Sizes C and D only –
Using C2, purl 1 row.

All Sizes –
Next Row: Using C2, K**14** (15-**7**-9), * K2tog, K**8** (8-**9**-9), rep from * to last **16** (17-**8**-10) sts, K2tog, knit to end … **272** (310-**314**-348) sts.
Work **17** (19-**19**-19) rows stocking st, beg with a purl row.

Next Row: Using C3, K**27** (30-**21**-25), * K2tog, K**6** (6-**7**-7), rep from * to last **29** (32-**23**-26) sts, K2tog, knit to end … **244** (278-**283**-314) sts.

Work **17** (19-**20**-20) rows stocking st, beg with a purl row.

Sizes C and D only –
Using C4, purl 1 row.

All Sizes –

Next Row: Using C4, K13 (14-**6**-8), * K2tog, K6 (6-**7**-7), rep from * to last **15** (16-**7**-9) sts, K2tog, knit to end … **216** (246-**252**-280) sts. Work **17** (19-**19**-19) rows stocking st, beg with a purl row.

Next Row: Using C5, K**26** (29-**20**-24), * K2tog, K4 (4-**5**-5), rep from * to last **28** (31-**22**-25) sts, K2tog, knit to end … **188** (214-**221**-246) sts. Work **17** (19-**20**-20) rows stocking st, beg with a purl row.

Sizes C and D only –
Using C6, purl 1 row.

All Sizes Proceed as Folls –
1st Row: Using C6, K**12** (13-**5**-7), * K2tog, K4 (4-**5**-5), rep from * to last **14** (15-**6**-8) sts, K2tog, knit to end … **160** (182-**190**-212) sts.

2nd and Foll Alt Rows: Purl.

3rd Row: K**37** (42-**44**-50), K2tog, K2, sl 1, K1, psso, knit to last **43** (48-**50**-56) sts, K2tog, K2, sl 1, K1, psso, knit to end … **156** (178-**186**-208) sts.

5th Row: K**36** (41-**43**-49), K2tog, K2, sl 1, K1, psso, knit to last **42** (47-**49**-55) sts, K2tog, K2, sl 1, K1, psso, knit to end.

7th Row: K**35** (40-**42**-48), K2tog, K2, sl 1, K1, psso, knit to last **41** (46-**48**-54) sts, K2tog, K2, sl 1, K1, psso, knit to end. Cont in this manner until **128** (146-**154**-176) sts rem.

Next Row: Purl.

Next Row: Using C7 for rem, K**10** (8-**1**-5), * K2tog, K1 (1-**3**-3), rep from * to last **10** (9-**3**-6) sts, K2tog, knit to end … **91** (102-**123**-142) sts. Work **11** (11-**5**-5) rows stocking st, beg with a purl row.

Sizes C and D only:

Next Row: K (**3**-7), * K2tog, K2, rep from * to last (**4**-7) sts, K2tog, knit to end … (**93**-109) sts. Work 5 rows stocking st, beg with a purl row.

All Sizes …
91 (102-**93**-109) sts.

Next Row: K**9** (8-**5**-6), * K**0** (0-**1**-1), rep from * to last **10** (8-**7**-7) sts, K2tog, knit to end … **54** (58-**65**-76) sts. Work **5** (7-**7**-7) rows stocking st, beg with a purl row.

Beg Neckband:

1st Row: Purl.

2nd Row: Knit.

3rd Row: Purl.
Cast off **loosely** knitways.

Front Bands (both alike):

Note: See knitting up stitches diagram on page 59.

With right side facing, using a **pair** of 4.00mm (US 6) needles and appropriate colour for each stripe, knit up **101** (101-**114**-114) sts evenly along front edge, incl side edge of neckband.
Keeping colours correct, proceed as folls:

1st Row (wrong side): Knit.

2nd Row: Purl.

3rd Row: Knit.

Cast off **loosely** purlways.
Rep for other front edge.

To Make up
Using C7 make 2 twisted cords **43** (46-**50**-50) cm or **17”** (18”-**19”**-19”) long.
Using C7, make 2 pompoms **5** (5-7.**5**-7.5) cm or **2”** (2”-**3”**-3”) diameter.
Attach twisted cords to ends of neckband and attach pompoms to ends of twisted cord.

heaps easy!

rainbow top

Measurements		Girl		Adult	
		A (yr)	B (yr)	C	D
		6-8	10-12	**8-10**	12-14
Finished Measurement:		**53cm**	63cm	**78cm**	88cm
		21"	24"	**30"**	34"
Length:		**26cm**	28cm	**42cm**	44cm
		10"	11"	**16"**	17"

Materials
Panda Disco 8 ply (20g balls)

	A	B	C	D
Main Colour	**3**	4	**6**	7
1st Contrast (C1)	**1**	1	**1**	1
2nd Contrast (C2)	**1**	1	**1**	1
3rd Contrast (C3)	**1**	1	**1**	1
4th Contrast (C4)	**1**	1	**1**	1
5th Contrast (C5)	**1**	1	**1**	1

One **pair** of 4.00mm (US 6) and a 4.00mm (US 6) **circular** knitting needle or the required size to give correct tension; 2 stitch holders; knitter's needle for sewing seams and embroidery.

Tension
This handknit has been designed at a tension of 22 sts and 30 rows to 10cm (4") over stocking st, using 4.00mm (US 6) needles.

looks tricky but its sooo.. easy!

Back and Front Alike

Using a **circular** 4.00mm (US 6) needle and MC, cast on **244** (284-**348**-396) sts.

Note: *A circular needle is used to accommodate the large number of sts, but work backwards and forwards in rows, not rounds.*

1st Row: * K2, sl first st over 2nd st, rep from * to end … **122** (142-**174**-198) sts.

2nd Row: * P2tog, rep from * to end … **61** (71-**87**-99) sts. Change to a **pair** of 4.00mm (US 6) needles and stocking st for rem.
Work **3** (3-**6**-6) row stripes in C1, C2, C3, C4 then C5. Using MC for rem, cont until work measures **9** (9-**22**-23) cm or **3"** (3"-**8"**-9") (from beg, ending with a purl row.

Shape Armholes:
Cast off **4** (6-**7**-8) sts at beg of next 2 rows … **53** (59-**73**-83) sts.
Dec one st at each end of next and foll alt rows until **45** (49-**61**-67) sts rem.
Work **9** (9-**7**-5) rows.

Divide for Strap:

Next Row: K8 (8-**12**-12), turn.
Cont on these **8** (8-**12**-12) sts until work measures
26 (28-**42**-44) cm or
10" (11"-**16"**-17") from beg, ending with a purl row.

Shape Shoulder:
Sizes C and D only:
Cast off 6 sts at beg of next row.
Work 1 row.

All Sizes:
Cast off rem **8** (8-**6**-6) sts.
Slip next **29** (33-**37**-43) sts onto a stitch holder and leave for neckband.
With right side facing, join yarn to rem **8** (8-**12**-12) sts, and cont until work measures same as other strap, ending with a purl row.
Knit 1 row.

Shape Shoulder:
Work as given for other shoulder shaping

Neckband

Join shoulder seams. With right side facing, using 4.00mm (US 6) **circular** needle and MC, beg at corner between back neck and left strap, ** knit up **49** (57 **57**-61) sts along entire strap to stitch holder, place a marker around first st on stitch holder (to indicate corner st), knit across sts on stitch holder to end, place a marker around last st from stitch holder (to indicate corner st) **, rep from ** to ** once … **156** (180-**188**-208) sts.

1st Round: * P2tog tbl, (K1, P1) to within 3 sts of corner st, K1, P2tog, K1 (corner st), rep from * 3 times …
148 (172-**180**-200) sts.

2nd Round: * P1, K1, rep from * to end.

3rd Round: * K2tog, rib to within 2 sts of corner st, sl 1, K1, psso, K1 (corner st), rep from * 3 times …
140 (164-**172**-192) sts.

4th Round: K1 * rib to within one st of corner st, K2, rep from * 3 times.

Cast off in rib.

Armhole Bands

With right side facing and using a **pair** of 4.00mm (US 6) needles and MC, knit up
83 (97-**109**-121) sts evenly around armhole edge.

1st Row: K1, * P1, K1, rep from * to end.

2nd Row: K2, * P1, K1, rep from * to last st, K1.
Rep last 2 rows once.
Cast off in rib.

To Make up
Join side and armhole band seams. Using "Knitting Stitch" and C1, embroider heart on front, working from Graph. 1 for sizes A and B, or Graph 2 for sizes C and D. Using MC, make a twisted cord **95** (105-**130**-140) cm or **37"** (41"-**51"**-55") long, thread through top of C5 stripe and tie in a bow.

Graph 1

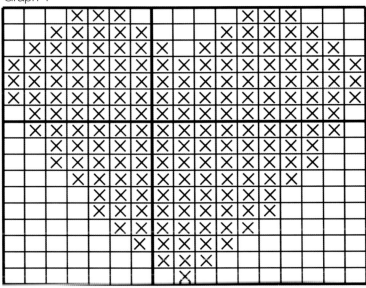

⟵ 17 sts ⟶

Graph 2

here are the heart patterns

⟵ 21 sts ⟶

☒ = Using C1 - 'Knitting St' embroidery

17

try this!

striped beanie

make your beanie in your favourite colours

Measurements

Measurements	A	B
To Fit Head:	**54**cm	56cm
	21"	22"
Length:	**20**cm	28cm
	8"	11"

Materials

Cleckheaton Merino Supreme
(50g balls)

	A	B
Main Colour (MC)	**2**	2
Contrast Colour (CC)	**1**	2

One **set** of 5.50mm (double-pointed US 9) knitting needles or the required size to give correct tension; hat elastic; knitter's needle for sewing in ends.

Tension

This handknit has been designed at a tension of 16 sts and 22 rows to 10cm (4") over stocking st, using 5.50mm (US 9) needles.

Using MC and a **set** of 5.50mm (double-pointed US 9) needles, cast on **64** (72) sts.

Note:
*When carrying colour for band, be sure to carry in **front** of work, **NOT** at back of work.*

Beg Fair Isle Band Patt
(See page 58 for help in working Fair Isle)

1st Round: * P2 MC, P2 CC, rep from * to end.

Beg Ribbed Patt:
2nd Round: * P2 MC, K2 CC, rep from * to end.
Rep 2nd round until band measures 10cm from beg.

Beg Stripe Patt:
Using CC, knit 6 rounds.
Using MC, knit 6 rounds.
Last 12 rounds form stripe patt for rem of hat.
Keeping stripe patt correct, cont until work measures **10** (14) cm or **4"**(5") from beg of stripe patt.

Shape Crown:
1st Round: Keeping stripes correct, * K2tog, **K6** (7), rep from * to end … 56 (64) sts.

2nd and Foll Alt Rounds: Knit.

3rd Round: * K2tog, **K5** (6), rep from * to end … **48** (56) sts.

5th Round: * K2tog, **K4** (5), rep from * to end … **40** (48) sts.

Cont dec in this manner in foll alt rounds until 16 sts rem.

Next Round: * K2tog, rep from * to end … 8 sts.

Break yarn, thread through rem sts, draw up and fasten off securely.

To Make up
Sew in ends. Turn up band.

poncho with armholes

easy as!

hey...
try this in one
colour with your
fave icon patch

Measurements

Measurements	Girl		Woman	
	A	B	C	D
To Fit Bust/Chest:	**65-70cm**	75-80cm	**75-80cm**	85-90cm
	25"-27"	29"-31"	**29"-31"**	33"-35"
Length:	**50cm**	55cm	**60cm**	61cm
	19"	21"	**23"**	24"

Materials
Cleckheaton Country 8 ply (50g balls)

	A	B	C	D
Main Colour (MC)	**8**	9	**10**	11
1st Contrast (C1)	**1**	1	**1**	1
2nd Contrast (C2)	**1**	1	**1**	1
3rd Contrast (C3)	**1**	1	**1**	1

One **pair** of 4.00mm (US 6) and a **set** of 4.00mm (double-pointed US 6) knitting needles or the required size to give correct tension; 2 stitch holders; knitter's needle for sewing seams and embroidery.

Tension
This handknit has been designed at a tension of 22 sts and 30 rows to 10cm (4") over stocking st, using 4.00mm (US 6) needles.

Back
Using a **pair** of 4.00mm (US 6) needles and MC, cast on **55** (71-**63**-73) sts.

1st Row: Knit.
2nd Row: Cast on **4** (4-**3**-3) sts, purl to end.

3rd Row: Cast on **4** (4-**3**-3) sts, knit to end … **63** (79-**69**-79) sts.
Rep last 2 rows **5** (5-**6**-6) times … **103** (119-**105**-115) sts.

Inc one st at each end of every row until there are **127** (143-**141**-151) sts, then in foll 6th rows until there are **133** (151-**151**-161) sts.
Place a marker at each end of last row to indicate beg of side seam.
Work 7 rows.
Place a marker at each end of last row to indicate beg of armholes.

Shape Armholes:
Dec one st at each end of every row until **127** (145-**145**-155) sts rem, then in foll alt rows until **121** (137-**139**-149) sts rem, then in foll 4th rows until **117** (133-**133**-143) sts rem.
Work 1 row.

Inc one st at each end of next and foll 4th row/s until there are **121** (137-**139**-149) sts, then in foll alt rows until there are **125** (145-**145**-155) sts, then in every row until there are **131** (151-**151**-161) sts.

Cast on **3** (3-**4**-4) sts at beg of next 2 rows … **137** (157-**159**-169) sts. **

Cont Side Shaping:
Dec one st at each end of next and foll alt rows until **83** (101-**109**-121) sts rem, then in every row until **65** (71-**71**-75) sts rem.

Shape Shoulders:
Cast off **6** (7-**6**-7) sts at beg of next 4 rows, then **6** (6-**7**-6) sts at beg of foll 2 rows.
Leave rem **29** (31-**33**-35) sts on a stitch holder.

Front
Work as given for Back to **.
Dec one st at each end of next and foll alt rows until **89** (103-**109**-121) sts rem, **Sizes C and D only** - then in every row until (**103**-111) sts rem.

Sizes A and B only - Purl 1 row.

All Sizes - Shape Neck:
1st Row: K2tog, **K35** (42-**41**-45), turn.
Cont on these **36** (43-**42**-46) sts for left side of neck.

Size S only - **2nd Row:** P2tog, purl to end.

3rd Row: K2tog, knit to last 2 sts, K2tog.

4th Row: Purl.

5th Row: As 3rd row … 31 sts.

Sizes B, C and D only - Dec one st at each end of next 2 rows … (39-**38**-42) sts.

All Sizes - Dec one st at side edge in every row **9** (13-**13**-15) times, **at same time** dec one st at neck edge in foll alt rows **4** (6-**6**-7) times … **18** (20-**19**-20) sts.

Shape Shoulder:
Cast off **6** (7-**6**-7) sts at beg of next and foll alt row.

Purl 1 row.
Cast off rem **6** (6-**7**-6) sts.
Slip next **15** (15-**17**-17) sts onto a stitch holder and leave.
Join MC to rem sts, knit to last 2 sts, K2tog.
Cont on these **36** (43-**42**-46) sts for right side of neck.

Size S only - 2nd Row:
Purl to last 2 sts, P2tog.

3rd Row: K2tog, knit to last 2 sts, K2tog.

4th Row: Purl.

5th Row: As 3rd row … 31 sts.

Sizes B, C and D only - Dec one st at each end of next 2 rows … (39-**38**-42) sts.

All Sizes - Dec one st at side edge in every row **9** (13-**13**-15) times, **at same time** dec one st at neck edge in foll alt rows **4** (6-**6**-7) times … **18** (20-**19**-20) sts. Knit 1 row.

Shape Shoulder:
Work as given for other shoulder.

Lower Bands
(Front and Back alike)
With right side facing, using 4.00mm needles and MC, knit up **161** (179-**181**-191) sts (see page 59 for help in knitting up stitches) evenly between lower markers.

1st Row (wrong side): Knit.

2nd Row: Purl.

3rd Row: Knit.
Cast off loosely purlways.

Neckband
Join side seams, noting to keep armholes open from markers to cast on sts.
With right side facing, using a **set** of 4.00mm (double-pointed US 6) needles and MC, beg at left shoulder seam, knit up **16** (17-**19**-20) sts evenly along left front neck shaping, knit across sts on front neck stitch holder, knit up **16** (17-**19**-20) sts evenly along right front neck shaping, then knit across sts on back neck stitch holder … **76** (80-**88**-92) sts.

1st Round: * K2, P2, rep from * to end.
Rep last round 5 times.
Cast off **loosely** in rib.

Armhole Bands
With right side facing, using a **set** of 4.00mm (double-pointed US 6) needles and MC, knit up **60** (64-**72**-72) sts evenly around armhole.
Work 6 rounds rib as given for Neckband.
Cast off **loosely** in rib.

To make up
NOTE: *We recommend you embroider the outlines of the hearts before filling in the remaining colour.*

Using 'Knitting Stitch' embroidery, embroider hearts on front of poncho, beg **14th** (30th-**44th**-44th) stocking st row.

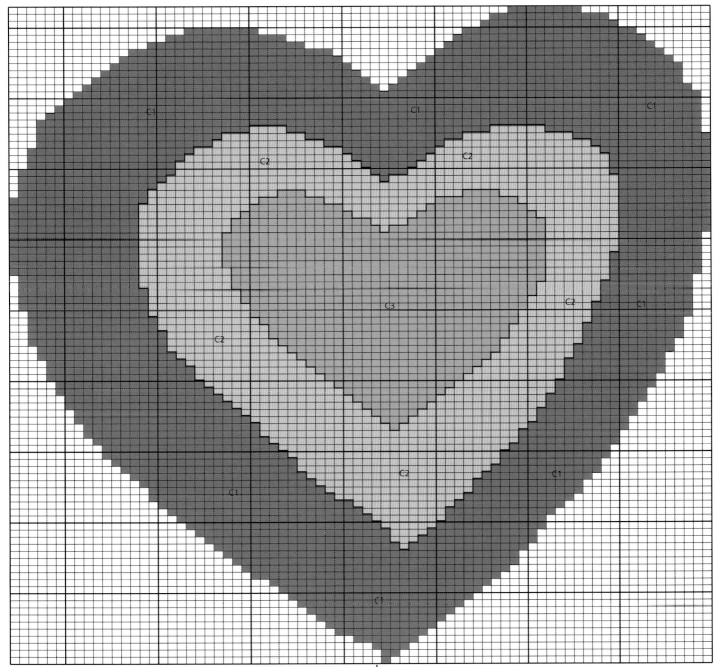

Centre stitch

23

heaps
easy!

snow bunny hat

Measurements

	Girl	Woman
To Fit Head:	**54cm**	56cm
	21"	22"

Materials
Cleckheaton Show Off
(50g balls)

Quantity	**5**	5 balls

One **pair** of 9.00mm (US 13) knitting needles or the required size to give correct tension; plain yarn and knitter's needle for sewing seams.

Tension
This handknit has been designed at a tension of 9 sts and 13 rows to 10cm (4") over stocking st, using 9.00mm (US 13) needles.

Hat
Using a **pair** of 9.00mm (US 13) needles, cast on **22** (24) sts.

1st Row: P2, * K2, P2, rep from * to last **0** (2) sts, K**0** (2).

2nd Row: K**2** (0), * P2, K2, rep from * to end.
Rep last 2 rows 3 times (8 rows in all).
Work **44** (56) rows stocking st.
Rep 1st and 2nd rows 4 times.
Cast off **loosely** in rib.

To Make up
Fold hat in half. Using plain yarn, sew side seams, reversing seam for 5cm (2") of rib to allow band to turn up. Make 2 pompoms 5cm (2") in diameter. Attach to tops of side seams.
Fold up band.

POMPOM SCARF

Measurements

Width:	17cm
	6"
Length:	126cm
	49"

Materials

Panda Magnum 8 ply
(100g balls)

1st Contrast (C1)	1
2nd Contrast (C2)	1
3rd Contrast (C3)	1
4th Contrast (C4)	1
5th Contrast (C5)	1
6th Contrast (C6)	1
7th Contrast (C7)	1

and Panda Woolbale 50 8 ply
(50g balls)

8th Contrast (C8)	1

Note: *Use only Panda Woolbale 50 for felting. Other yarns may not felt.*

One **pair** of 4.00mm (US 6) knitting needles or the required size to give correct tension; sewing needle and matching thread for attaching hearts; knitter's needle for darning ends.

Tension

This handknit has been designed at a tension of 33 sts and 30 rows to 10cm (4") over rib, using 4.00mm (US 6) needles.

Scarf

Using 4.00mm (US 6) needles and C1, cast on 56 sts.

1st Row: * K1, P1, rep from * to end.
Last row forms rib patt for scarf.
Work a further 53 rows rib.
Work 54 rows rib in each of C2, C3, C4, C5, C6 and C7.
Using C7, cast off in rib.

Knitted Rectangle

(for felted hearts)

Using 4.00mm (US 6) needles and C8, cast on 55 sts.
Work in stocking st until work measures 25cm (approx. 10") from beg.

Cast off.

To Make up

Felt rectangle. Using template, cut 2 heart shapes from rectangle and sew to each end of scarf (as illustrated). Make 2 pompoms (each 4cm or 1" diameter) in each of C1, C2 and C3. Make 1 pompom (each 4cm 0r 1" diameter) in each of C4, C5, C6 and C7. Using C1, make 5 twisted cords, each comprising 4 strands 25cm (10") long. Thread twisted cords evenly along cast on edge. On 1st, 3rd and 5th cord, tie a knot 7cm (3") down. On 2nd and 4th cord, tie a knot 5cm (2") (down. Attach a pompom to each cord, just below the knot. Thread all ends through pompom and trim neatly. Using C7, rep along cast off edge.

inca hat

easy
as!

Measurements	A	B
To Fit Head:	**54cm**	56cm
	21"	22"
Length:	**18cm**	24cm
	7"	9"

Materials
Cleckheaton Gusto 10
(100g balls)

Main Colour (MC)	2	2
Contrast Colour (CC)	1	2

(One **set** of 7.00mm (double-pointed US 10) knitting needles or the required size to give correct tension; knitter's needle for sewing in ends.

Tension
This handknit has been designed at a tension of 10 sts and 16 rows to 10cm (4") over stocking st, using 7.00mm (US 10) needles.

Ear Flaps (make 2)
Using two of the **set** of 7.00mm (double-pointed US 10) needles and CC, cast on **7** (8) sts.

Work **8** (10) rows stocking st.

Break off yarn and leave sts on a stitch holder for Flap A and leave yarn attached for Flap B.

Hat
Using CC and 7.00mm (double-pointed US 10) needles, with right side facing, knit across Flap B, cast on **14** (16) sts and with right side facing knit across Flap A … **28** (32) sts.

Purl 1 row.

Using MC, work **2** (3) rows stocking st.

Using CC, work **4** (5) rows stocking st.

Leave these **28** (32) sts on needle for next instruction.

NOTE: *You will now be working in rounds, not rows.*

Using all needles in a **set** of 7.00mm (double-pointed US 10) needles, and CC, cast on **20** (22) sts, knit across **28** (32) sts, making sure to divide all sts evenly around 3 needles as you knit … **48** (54) sts.
Knit 3 rounds.
Using MC, knit **12** (13) rounds.

Shape Crown:
1st Round: Using CC, * K2tog, K4, rep from * to end … **40** (45) sts.
Knit **1** (3) round/s.

Next Round: * K2tog, K3, rep from * to end … **32** (36) sts.
Knit **1** (3) round/s.

Next Round: * K2tog, K2, rep from * to end … **24** (27) sts.
Knit **1** round.
Using MC, knit 3 rounds.

Next Round: Using CC, * K2tog, K1, rep from * to end … **16** (18) sts.
Knit **1** (3) round/s.

Next Round: * K2tog, rep from * to end … **8** (9) sts.

Break off yarn, run end through rem sts, draw up tightly and fasten off securely.

To make up
Using MC make 3 pompoms, 6.5cm (3") in diameter (refer page 57). Using CC, make 2 twisted cords (refer page 59) 10 cm (4") in length and attach one to end of each ear flaps. Attach one pompom to top of hat and one to end of each twisted cord end.

Measurements

	Girl	Woman
To Fit Hand:	15cm	18.5cm
	6"	7"

Materials

Cleckheaton Country 8 ply
(50g balls)

1st Colour (C1 - pink)	**1**	1
2nd Colour (C2 - aqua)	**1**	1

and Panda Woolbale 50 8 ply
(50g balls)

small quantities of corresponding colours (C3 and C4) for felting

One pair of 4.00mm (US 6) knitting needles or the required size to give correct tension; cardboard or pompom maker; knitter's needle for sewing seams and embroidery.

Tension

This handknit has been designed at a tension of 22 sts and 30 rows to 10cm (4") over stocking st, using 4.00mm (US 6) needles.

easy
as!

mittens

Right Mitten

Using 4.00mm (US 6) needles and C1 (pink),
cast on **38** (42) sts.

Beg Rib:
1st Row: K2, * P2, K2,
rep from * to end.

2nd Row: P2, * K2, P2,
rep from * to end.
Rep last 2 rows 5 times
(12 rows rib in all).
Work 2 rows stocking st.

Increase for Thumb:
1st Row: K22 (24), place
marker for beg of thumb sts,
inc in each of next 2 sts, place
marker for end of thumb sts,
knit to end … **40** (44) sts.

** 2nd Row: Purl.

3rd Row: Knit to 1st marker,
inc in next st, knit to within one
st of next marker, inc in next st,
knit to end.

4th Row: Purl.
Rep last 2 rows **4** (5) times …
50 (56) sts.

Work Thumb:
1st Row: Knit to 2nd marker, **turn**.

2nd Row: Cast on one st,
purl to other marker,
turn … 15 (17) sts.
Cont on these **15** (17) sts for
thumb.
Cast on one st at beg of next
row … **16** (18) sts.
Work **9** (11) rows stocking st.

Shape top of Thumb:
Next Row: K1 (0), * K2tog, K1,
rep from * to end … 11 (12) sts.
Purl 1 row.

Next Row: K1 (0), * K2tog,
rep from * to end … 6 sts.
Break off yarn, leaving an end
about 25cm (10") long.
Thread through rem 6 sts,
draw up tightly and fasten off
securely. Sew thumb seam.

Work Hand:
With right side facing, join yarn
to hand sts, knit up 2 sts from
sts cast on for thumb, knit to
end … **38** (42) sts.
Work in stocking st until work
measures **6** (9) cm **2"** (3") from
base of thumb, ending with a
purl row.

Shape Top:
1st Row: K2, * K2tog, K7 (8),
rep from * to end … **34** (38) sts.

2nd and Foll Alt Rows: Purl.

3rd Row: K2, * K2tog, K6 (7),
rep from * to end … **30** (34) sts.
Cont dec in this manner,
working one st less between dec
in foll alt rows until 22 sts rem.

Next Row: * P2tog, rep from *
to end … 11 sts.
Break off yarn, draw end
through rem sts and secure
firmly. Fasten off.

Left Mitten
Using 4.00mm (US 6) needles &
C2 (aqua), cast on **38** (42) sts.

Beg Rib:
1st Row: K2, * P2, K2,
rep from * to end.

2nd Row: P2, * K2, P2,
rep from * to end.
Rep last 2 rows 5 times
(12 rows rib in all).
Work 2 rows stocking st.

Increase for Thumb:
1st Row: K14 (16), place
marker for beg of thumb sts,
inc in each of next 2 sts, place
marker for end of thumb sts,
knit to end … **40** (44) sts.
Complete as given for Right
Mitten from ** to end.

First Heart
Using 4.00mm (US 6) needles
and C4, cast on 30 sts.
Work in stocking st until work
measures 14cm (5") from beg.
Cast off.

Second Heart
Using C3, work as given for first
heart.

Finishing Mittens
Sew hand seam. Felt hearts and
cut out using template.
Make a 20cm (8") long twisted
cord in each of C1 and C2.
Attach twisted cords to wrists of
same colour mittens.
Make a pompom in each of C1
and C2 and attach to other end
of twisted cord. Using 'Blanket
St' (see page 59) sew hearts on
contrasting mittens.

heaps
easy!

scarf

34

with pocket

hey look! a
pocket for
your mobile
phone or
lipgloss

35

Measurements

Scarf measures (approx, excluding fringes): 15 x 152cm

6" x 61"

Materials

Cleckheaton Country 8 ply
(50g balls)

Main Colour (MC - aqua)	2
1st Contrast (C1 - punch)	1
2nd Contrast (C2 - lolly pink)	1
3rd Contrast (C3 - purple)	1
4th Contrast (C4 - orange)	1
5th Contrast (C5 - green)	1

One **pair** of 4.00mm (US 6) knitting needles or the required size to give correct tension; 1 button (or make knitted button see page 47); cardboard and crochet hook for fringe; knitter's needle for seam and sewing in ends.

Tension

This scarf has been designed at a tension of 22 sts and 30 rows to 10cm (4") over stocking st, using 4.00mm (US 6) needles.

Scarf

Using 4.00mm (US 6) needles and MC, cast on 37 sts.

1st Row: K4, P2, knit to last 6 sts, P2, K4.

2nd Row: P4, K2, purl to last 6 sts, K2, P4.
Last 2 rows form patt. **
Work a further 44 rows patt.
Cast off one st at beg of next 2 rows ... 35 sts.
Keeping patt correct, work in stripes as folls:
Using C1, work 14 rows.
Using C2, work 8 rows.
Using C3, work 24 rows.
Using C2, work 14 rows.
Using C4, work 12 rows.
Using C5, work 24 rows.
Using MC, work 12 rows.
Using C2, work 30 rows.
Using C4, work 14 rows.
Using C1, work 14 rows.
Using MC, work 36 rows.
Using C2, work 8 rows.
Using C5, work 30 rows.
Using C1, work 14 rows.
Using C2, work 12 rows.
Using C4, work 24 rows.
Using C2, work 12 rows.
Using MC, work 14 rows.
Using C1, work 8 rows.
Using C2, work 24 rows.
Using C5, work 14 rows.
Using MC, work 12 rows.
Using C1, work 30 rows.
Cast off.

Pocket

Work as given for Scarf to **.
Work a further 38 rows patt.

Next Row (buttonhole row): Patt 17, yfwd (to make a st), K2tog, patt to end.
Work 1 row, dec one st in centre ... 36 sts.

Next Row: K3, * P2, K2, rep from * to last st, K1.

Next Row: P3, * K2, P2, rep from * to last st, P1.
Rep last 2 rows twice (6 rows rib in all).
Cast off in rib.

Button (optional, make 1)

Using 4.00mm (US 6) needles and C2, cast on one st.

1st Row: (Knit into front and back of st) 3 times ... 6 sts.

2nd Row: (K1, P1) 3 times. Rep last row 3 times.

6th Row: Sl 3, K3tog, p3sso. Fasten off.

To make up

Note: *We recommend using 'Mattress St' to sew on the pocket (refer page 58).*

Sew pocket to beg of scarf.
Sew on button. Sew in ends.
Wind C4 around a piece of cardboard 8cm (3") wide and cut along one edge.
Using hook and 4 strands of yarn, fold yarn in half and draw loop through first st at cast on edge.
Draw ends through and tighten.
Rep along cast on edge. Using C2, work similar fringe at cast off edge. Trim fringes neatly.

whats your fave colour combo?

heaps
easy!

star top

Measurements	Girl	Girl	Adult	Adult
	A	B	C	D
	6-8	10-12	8-10	12-14
Finished Measurement:	**62cm**	73cm	**73cm**	89cm
	24"	28"	**28"**	35"
Length (at side seam):	**12cm**	14cm	**24cm**	26cm
	4"	5"	**9"**	10"

Materials
Panda Disco 8 ply (20g balls)

Main Colour	**3**	3	**4**	4
1st Contrast (C1)	**1**	1	**2**	2
2nd Contrast (C2)	**1**	1	**1**	1

One **pair** of 4.00mm (US 6) knitting needles and a 4.00mm (US 6) **circular** knitting needle or the required size to give correct tension; 2 stitch holders; hat elastic; knitter's needle for sewing seams and embroidery.

Tension
This handknit has been designed at a tension of 22 sts and 30 rows to 10cm (4") over stocking st, using 4.00mm (US 6) needles.

> how fab would this look made with a glittery yarn?

Back

Using a **pair** of 4.00mm (US 6) needles and C1, cast on 68 (80-**80**-98) sts.

1st Row: K3, * P2, K4, rep from * to last 5 sts, P2, K3.

2nd Row: P3, * K2, P4, rep from * to last 5 sts, K2, P3. Rep last 2 rows 2 (3-5-5) times. Using MC for rem, work 24 (24-**48**-54) rows stocking st. Leave sts on a stitch holder.

Front

Work until there are 2 rows less than Back to end, ending with a purl row.

Beg Turnings:

Note: *When turning, take yarn under needle and onto other side of work, slip next st onto right hand needle, take yarn under needle and back to original position, slip st back onto left hand needle, then turn and proceed as instructed. This avoids holes in work.*

1st and 2nd Rows: Work to last **10** (11-**6**-12) sts, **turn**.

3rd and 4th Rows: Work to last **15** (18-**11**-17) sts, **turn**.

5th and 6th Rows: Work to last **20** (25-**16**-22) sts, **turn**.

Sizes C and D only -

7th and 8th Rows: Work to last (**21**-27) sts, **turn**.

9th and 10th Rows: Work to last (**26**-32) sts, **turn**.

All Sizes -
Next Row: Knit to end.

Next Row: Purl across all sts. Leave sts on a stitch holder.

Top Band

Join side seams. With right side facing, using 4.00mm (US 6) **circular** needle and C1, [K2tog, knit to last 2 sts, K2tog] across back stitch holder, then [K2tog, knit to last 2 sts, K2tog] across front stitch holder … **132** (156-**156**-192) sts.

1st Round: K2, * P2, K4 rep from * to last 4 sts, P2, K2. Rep 1st round **4** (6-**10**-10) times. Cast off in rib.

To make up

Using "Knitting Stitch", C1 and C2, embroider stars on front, working from Graph 1 for sizes A and B or Graph 2 for sizes C and D, beg **4** (4-**4**-7) rows above lower band. Thread thin elastic through first and last rows of top and bottom bands.

Graph 1

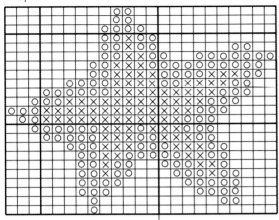

Centre of front

star patterns

☒ = Using C1 - 'Knitting St' embroidery
◯ = Using C2 - 'Knitting St' embroidery

Graph 2

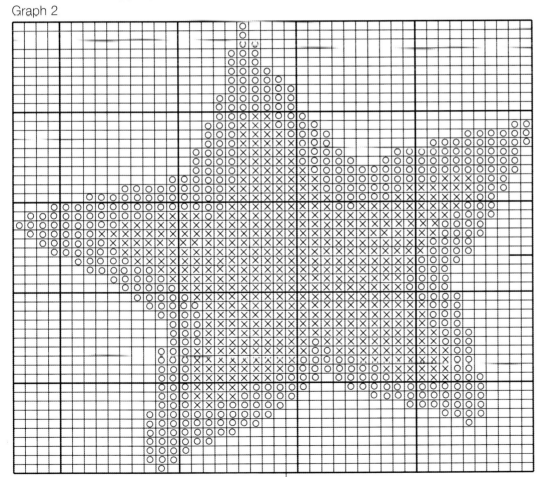

Centre of front

heaps easy!

hooded scarf

Measurements

To Fit Head:	**54cm**	56cm
	21"	22"
Width:	**21cm**	26cm
	8"	10"
Length:	**150cm**	190cm
	59"	76"
Pocket Length:	**13cm**	17cm
	5"	6"

Materials
Cleckheaton Angora Supreme
(50g balls)

Quantity	**4**	6

One **pair** of 4.50mm (US 7) knitting needles or the required size to give correct tension; knitter's needle for sewing seams.

Tension
This handknit has been designed at a tension of 19 sts and 28 rows to 10 cm (4") over stocking st, using 4.50mm (US 7) needles.

Scarf

Beg at pocket edge:
Using 4.50mm (US 7) needles, cast on **42** (52) sts.

1st Row: Knit
(1st row is wrong side).

2nd Row: Purl.

3rd Row: Knit.
Work 33 (45) rows stocking st (beg with knit row).

Next Row: Knit (pocket ridge).
Work a further **36** (48) rows In stocking st (beg with knit row).
Tie a marker at each end of last row.

Beg scarf patt:

1st Row: P3, K2,
purl to last 5 sts, K2, P3.

2nd Row: K3, P2,
knit to last 5 sts, P2, K3.
Last 2 rows form rib patt for scarf.

Rep last 2 rows until work measures **42** (56) cm from markers (ending with a 1st row). Place a 2nd set of markers at each end of last row.

Beg Hood patt:
1st Row: K3, P2, knit to end.

2nd Row: Purl to last 5 sts, K2, P3.
Last 2 rows form patt for Hood. Rep last 2 rows until work measures **16** (18) cm or **6"** (7") from 2nd markers, ending with a 2nd row of patt.

Shape Hood Top:
1st Row: Patt to last 2 sts, K2tog.

2nd Row: P2tog, patt to end.

3rd Row: Patt to last 2 sts, K2tog … **39** (49) sts.

4th Row: Patt to end.
Rep last 4 rows twice … **33** (43) sts.

Next Row: Patt to end.

Next Row: Inc in next st, patt to end.

Next Row: Patt to last st, inc in last st.

Next Row: Inc in next st, patt to end … **36** (46) sts.
Rep last 4 rows twice … **42** (52) sts.

Cont Hood patt (beg with 1st row) until work measures **40** (44) cm or **15"** (17") from 2nd markers (ending with a 2nd row of patt).
Tie a 3rd set of markers at each end of last row.
Work in Scarf patt (beg with a 2nd row) until work measures **42** (56) cm or **16"** (22") from 3rd markers, ending with a 2nd row.
Work 36 (48) rows stocking st (beg with a knit row).
Purl 1 row (pocket ridge).
Work 33 (45) rows stocking st (beg with a purl row).

Next Row: Purl.

Next Row: Knit.

Next Row: Purl.
Cast off.

To make up
Fold scarf in half (2nd and 3rd markers will meet for hood).
Sew back seam of hood.
Fold up pockets along ridge, sew up sides of pockets.

trick up your
scarf with
icon patches

butterfly bag

heaps
easy!

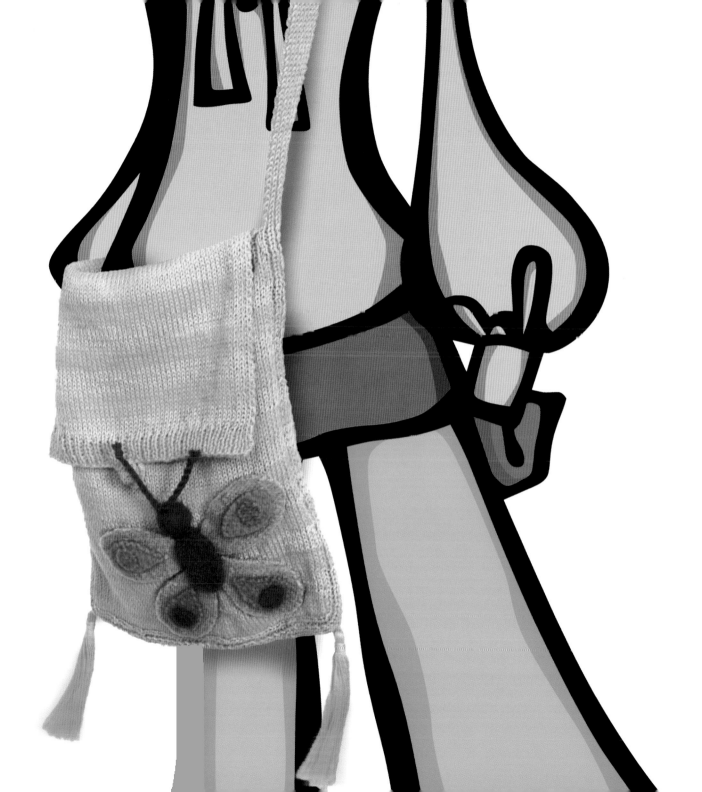

Measurements

Bag with long strap (approx):	23 x 78cm
	9" x 30"
Bag with short strap (approx):	23 x 58cm
	9" x 23"

Materials

Panda Regal 4 ply (50g balls)

Main Colour (MC)	2
Contrast Colour (CC)	1

And **Panda Woolbale 50 8ply** (50g balls) for butterfly (see page 61).

One **pair** of 3.25mm (US 3) knitting needles or the required size to give correct tension; knitter's needle for sewing seams.

Tension

This bag has been designed at a tension of 27 sts and 34 rows to 10cm (4") over stocking st, using 3.25mm (US 3) needles.

Front of Bag

Using 3.25mm (US 3) needles and MC, cast on 65 sts.
Work 6 rows stocking st.
Using CC, work 6 rows stocking st.
Last 12 rows form stripe patt.
Cont in stripe patt until work measures approx 26cm (10") from beg, ending with 6 rows in MC. **

Next Row: Using CC, K2, * P1, K1, rep from * to last st, K1.

Next Row: K1, * P1, K1, rep from * to end.
Rep last 2 rows twice.
Cast off loosely.

Back of Bag

Work as given for front of bag to **.
Using CC, work 6 rows stocking st.
Tie a marker at each end of last row, to mark beg of flap.

Next Row: Using MC, K1, (K1, P1) twice, knit to last 5 sts, (P1, K1) twice, K1.

Next Row: K1, (P1, K1) twice, purl to last 5 sts, (K1, P1) twice, K1.
Rep last 2 rows twice.

Next Row: Using CC, K1, (K1, P1) twice, knit to last 5 sts, (P1, K1) twice, K1.

Next Row: K1, (P1, K1) twice, purl to last 5 sts, (K1, P1) twice, K1.

Rep last 2 rows twice.

Rep last 12 rows until work measures approx 12cm (4") from markers, ending with 6 rows in CC.

Next Row: Using MC, K2, * P1, K1, rep from * to last st, K1.

Next Row: K1, * P1, K1, rep from * to end.

Rep last 2 rows twice.

Cast off loosely in rib.

Long Strap

Using 3.25mm (US 3) needles and MC, cast on 15 sts.

1st Row: K2, * P1, K1, rep from * to last st, K1.

1st Row: * K1, P1, rep from * to end.

Rep last 2 rows twice.

Using CC, work 6 rows rib.

Last 12 rows form stripe patt for strap. Cont in stripe patt until strap measures approx 28cm (11") from beg, ending with 6 rows in CC.

Tie a marker at each end of last row (this will help with sewing up the bag). **

Using MC only, cont in rib until work measures 101cm (40") from marker.

*** Tie a marker at each end of last row.

Work in stripe patt until work measures approx 28cm (11") from second marker, ending with 6 rows in MC.

Tie a marker at each end of last row.

Cont in stripe patt until work measures approx 23cm (9") from third marker, ending with 6 rows in CC.

Cast off in rib.

Short Strap

Work as given for long strap to **.

Using MC only, cont in rib until work measures 61cm (24") from marker.

Work as given for long strap from *** to end.

Knitted Button

Using 3.25mm (US 3) needles and CC, cast on 1 st.

1st Row: Knit into front, back, front, then back of st ... 4 sts.

2nd Row: (Inc in next st) 4 times ... 8 sts.

Work 7 rows stocking st (beg with a purl row).

10th Row: (K2tog) 4 times ... 4 sts.

11th Row: K4tog Fasten off.

Gather edges into a ball and fill with scrap yarn before fastening securely.

To make up

Sew cast on and cast off edges of strap tog, forming a circle. Sew strap to front and back of bag, noting that cast on edge to first marker fits along one side of bag, second to third marker fits along other side of bag and third marker to cast off edge fits along base of bag. Fold flap over. Using MC, make 2 tassels each 11cm (4") long and attach to corners of bag. To make button loop, using MC, make 2 loops on centre edge of flap. Work 'Buttonhole St' over loops. Sew on knitted button to correspond with loop. Make a butterfly (see page 61) and attach as illustrated.

how to knit info

making a slip knot

1 The slip knot becomes the first stitch. Grab the cut end of the yarn in your palm with your thumb. Wind the yarn from the ball twice around your index and middle fingers.

....so far so easy....

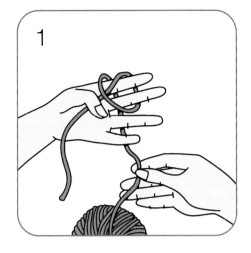

2 Pull the yarn belonging to the ball through the loop between your two fingers, creating a new loop.

Get it?

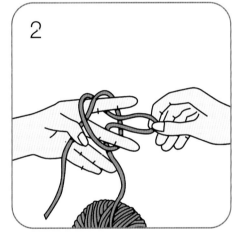

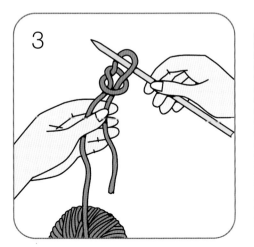

3 Now put the new loop on the needle. Tighten by pulling on both ends of the yarn to form the slip knot. To get ready for casting on, be sure to leave extra length when making the slip knot.

Too cool, you've done it.

casting on

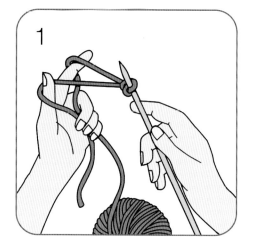

1 Put the needle with the slip knot in your right hand, then wind the cut end around your left thumb. Wow! Wrap yarn from the ball over left index finger. Grab ends in your palm.

Are you following?

2 Poke the needle upwards in the loop on your thumb, then behind the loop on your index finger - cool! Now using the needle draw the yarn up from the ball through the loop to form a stitch.

You are nearly there!

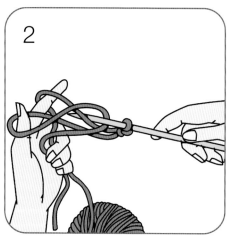

3 Move your thumb out of the loop and pull the cut end to tighten the stitch on the needle. Repeat steps 1 to 3 until the desired number of stitches are cast on.

Fabo!

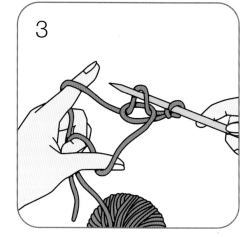

making a knit stitch

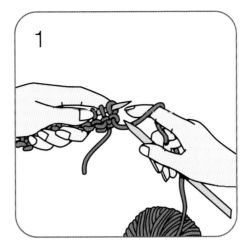

1 Place the needle with the stitch in your left hand, the first stitch is near the tip. Grab the empty needle in your right hand, wind the yarn around your fingers as you see in the picture. Stick the right needle from front to back into the first stitch on the left needle. Leave the right needle under the left needle and the yarn at the back. Do you have it right?

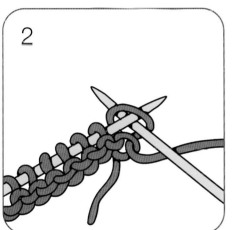

2 Pull the right needle from front to back into the first stitch on the left needle. Keep the right needle under the left needle and the yarn at the back.

3 Grab and pull the yarn under and over the right needle, and pull it softly between the two needles. Using your right index finger to control the yarn.

Doing well!

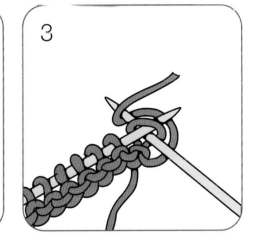

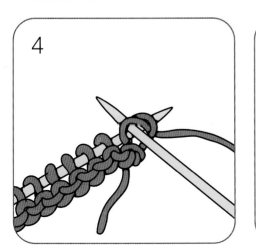

4 Grab the right needle, hook onto the yarn and pull it through the stitch on the left needle. Now slip the stitch off the left needle, leaving the new stitch on the right. Repeat steps 2 to 4 until all the new stitches are on the right needle.

See it's too easy!

making a purl stitch

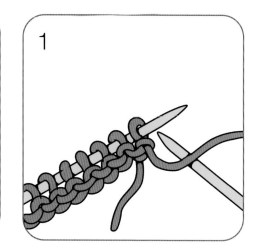

1 The needle with the stitches has to be in your left hand and the empty needle in your right hand. When creating the purl stitch, the yarn is held to the front of the work. Insert the right needle from back to front into the first stitch. The right needle is now in front of the left needle, and the yarn is at the front of your work.

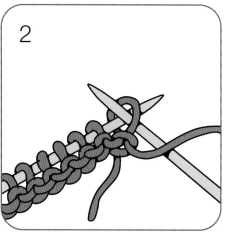

2 Put the right needle from back to front into the first stitch. The right needle should be in front of the left needle, and the yarn is at the front of your work.

3 Use your right index finger, wind the yarn counter-clockwise around the right needle in a downward direction as picture.

Rockin.....

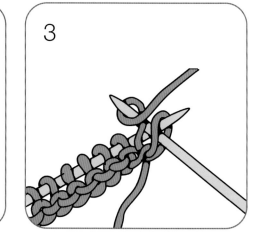

4 Bring backwards the right needle and yarn through the stitch on the left needle, making a loop on the right needle. Slip the stitch off the left needle. Repeat steps 2 to 4 until all the new stitches are all on the right needle.

Too easy!

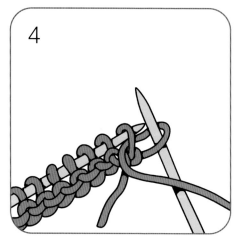

... and more

Changing the Yarn

Knit to the end of a row. Cut the yarn leaving an end about 15cm (6") long. Knit a few more stitches with the new yarn leaving a 15cm (6") end and tie the two ends together.

Stocking (Stockinette) Stitch

Knit the first row. Then purl the second row , repeat the first and second rows.

Rib

Knit 1, purl 1 right across the rows.

Decreasing (for knitwise)

On the knit row, knit 2 stitches together.

Decreasing (purlwise)

On the purl row, purl 2 stitches together. Put the RH needle through 2 stitches and purl as usual. You can decrease at the beginning, middle or end of a row. To lose more than one stitch, carry on knitting or purling 2 stitches together.

Increasing (knitwise)

On a knit row, knit the stitch as usual but do not drop the stitch off the needle.

Increasing (purlwise)

On the purl row, purl the stitch as usual but do not drop the stitch off the needle. You can increase at the beginning, middle or end of a row.

checking tension or gauge

Sometimes the size of a finished project doesn't really matter - a scarf can be a bit wider and it will be just as cool to wear.

But if you are creating a groovy poncho, you will want it to finish up the right size for a fab fit. You will hate that it is too big and gets longer every time you wear it. Mega bad is a poncho that is too small for you to even try it on. This means get serious about the word 'tension'.

When the finished size matters, the pattern will have a tension listed near the materials and measurements panel.

Tension is stated as a number of sts to 10cm (4"), along with suggested needle size and the stitch/pattern to use. You will need to get this tension for your project to be the size listed in the pattern.

It will save a lot of agony later if you check your tension before you begin your project.

To check your tension, be sure to knit a sample.

Using the suggested needles, cast on about 1.5 times the number of sts stated in the tension.

Work in the stitch/pattern stated until the sample is a square. Cast off loosely.

Measure across 10cm (4") in the middle of the square and count how many sts there are (each V shape is one st). Compare this with the number stated in the pattern

If you do not have enough sts, your tension is loose and you should knit another square using needles one size smaller.

If you have too many sts, your tension is way tight and you should knit another square using needles one size larger.

Measure 10cm (4") and count the sts as before.

Keep changing needles and knitting another square until you get the right number.

When you have the correct number of sts, you are cool to start knitting your pattern.

casting off or binding off

When you have finished knitting your project, you need to finish off the edges so it all stays together without unravelling.

1 Knit two stitches. *Put the left-hand (LH) needle into the first stitch on the right needle.

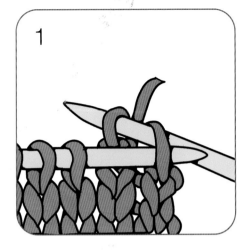

2 Grab and pull this stitch over the second stitch and off the right-hand (RH) needle.

3 One stitch remains on the right needle as shown. Knit the next stitch. Repeat from the * in step 1 until you have bound off the required number of stitches. When one stitch remains on the RH needle, pull the yarn through the loop to fasten off.

You have mastered it!

abbreviations

alt = alternate;
approx = approximately;
beg = begin/ning;
cm = centimetres;
cont = continue;
dec = decrease, decreasing;
foll = follows, following;
garter st = every row knit;
inc = increase, increasing;
incl = inclusive, including;
K = Knit;
'M1' = make 1 - pick up loop which lies before next st, place on left hand needle and knit into back of loop;
0 = (zero) - no sts, rows or times;
P = Purl;
patt = pattern;
psso = pass slipped st over;
p2sso = pass 2 slipped sts over;
p3sso = pass 3 slipped sts over;

purl fabric (reverse stockinette) (wrong side of stocking st) = purl right side rows and knit wrong side rows;
rem = remain/ing;
rep = repeat;
sl = slip;
st/s = stitch/es;
stocking st (st st) = 1 row knit, 1 row purl;
tbl = through back of loop;
tog = together;
ybk = yarn back - take yarn under needle from purling position into knitting position, without making a st;
yft (wyif) = yarn front - bring yarn under needle from knitting position into purling position, without making a st;
yfwd (yo) = yarn forward - bring yarn under needle, then over into knitting position again, making a st;
yon = yarn over needle - take yarn over top of needle into knitting position, making a st;
yrn = yarn round needle - take yarn right around needle into purling position, making a st.

When instructions read - 'Cast off 2 sts, K5 (or another number), the st left on the right hand needle after casting off, counts as one st.

knitting needles

US	METRIC
0	2.00mm
1	2.25mm
2	2.50mm
2	3.00mm
3	3.25mm
4	3.50mm
5	3.75mm
6	4.00mm
7	4.50mm
8	5.00mm
9	5.50mm
10	6.50mm
10 1/2	6,7,7.5mm
11	8.00mm
13	9.00mm
15	10.00mm
17	12.75mm
19	15.00mm
35	19mm

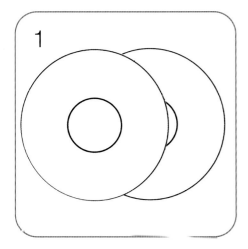

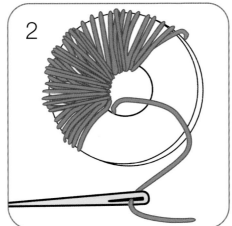

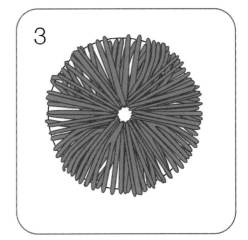

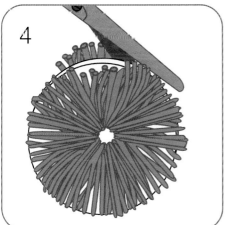

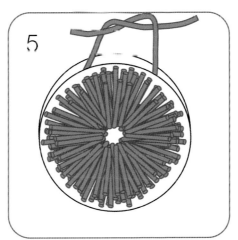

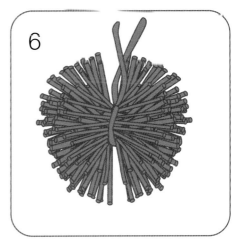

pompoms

1 Cut out two circles from cardboard (size stated on pattern) and cut out holes in the centre.

2 Put the circles together and wrap the yarn round and round!

3 Don't stop until the hole is filled in.

4 Cut the yarn around the edge of the two circles.

5 Pull the circles apart slightly and wrap yarn in between and make a firm knot.

6 Pull the circles off and trim the pompom to neaten.

Hey cool you made a pompom!

Knitting Stitch Embroidery

1 Begin by pulling the needle up in the centre of the first stitch and take it up and around the head of the stitch from right to left.

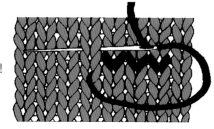

2 Put the needle back through the centre of the original stitch and out through the centre of the stitch on the left. Not sure – look at the diagram!

3 Just remember when you work back the other way do the opposite!

Fair Isle

This is when two colours are knitted in the same row. Start knitting with colour 1 and keep colour 2 on the wrong side. All you do is pick up colour 2 when the pattern says!

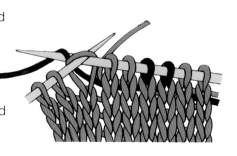

Always take both colours to the end of the row and twist together before beginning the next row. It's a bit hard but you can do it!

Set of Needles

A set of needles is four or more needles with points on both ends. If you want to knit without seams these are great to use. You put the stitches on three of the needles and use the fourth needle to knit with.

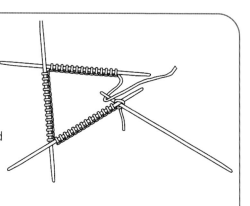

As you knit, the free needle will change over. Cool you are knitting in a circle!

Mattress Stitch

Hey this is a cool stitch to learn! It is almost invisible so it is great to use it to sew up your projects.

1 Put the two edges of your project together, right sides showing.

2 Use matching yarn and make a stitch leaving a long end.

3 Put the needle between the edge stitch and the second stitch on the first row. Push the needle under two rows and then bring back through to the front.

4 Repeat on the other piece and keep swapping from side to side. Remember to always go into the hole that the last stitch on that side came out of!

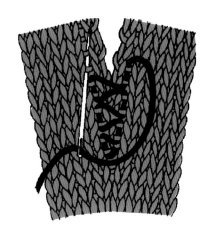

Twisted Cord

1 Knot the pieces of yarn together at each end.

2 Attach one end to something to hold it in place, insert a knitting needle though the other end. Keep twisting the needle until the yarns are well twisted!

3 Grab the centre of the yarns. Place the two ends together, but make sure you keep it tight.

4 Let go of the centre of the yarns, watch the two pieces twist together – cool! Knot both ends.

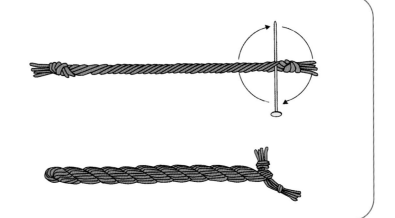

Buttonhole (Blanket) Stitch

1 Make a couple of long stitches where you want a button loop.

2 Stitch over these long stitches with buttonhole stitch – look at the diagram. Push the stitches up tight as you go.

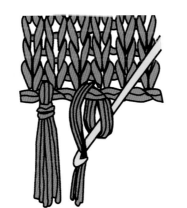

Fringes

Cut a piece of cardboard to the length of fringe you want. Wind yarn round and round. Cut along one edge. Fold the yarns in half and pull the loop through a stitch on the end of your project. Pull the ends through the loop to form a knot.

Hey your first fringe, now keep going!

Knitting Up Stitches

1 Put your needle through the second stitch from the edge. Wrap yarn around the needle and pull back through.

2 That makes one stitch!

3 Repeat step 1 along the edge of your knitting until all stitches are knitted up! Wow! now you can begin knitting.

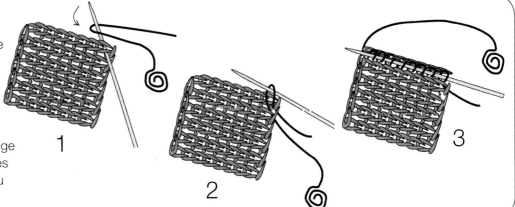

felt icon patches

hey this is so cool to make your own icon patches! felting is fun and easy to do and you can make up your own groovy designs

felting by hand

You will need a bowl, a piece of knitting, laundry soap and rubber gloves.

Wearing the rubber gloves, put the knitting into the bowl and add enough hot water to cover the knitting. Let it sit for a few minutes.

Add enough cold water so you can put your hands in the water (it still needs to be hot). Rub soap into the knitting.

Bunch the knitting in your hands and rub it against itself, creating friction. Keep moving the knitting around, Occasionally dunk in the water. Do this for about 5 minutes.

Rinse the knitting in cold water. Repeat the entire process twice more then check how well your knitting has felted. If you can still see the stitches, repeat the entire process again.

Wow your felted knitting can now be cut without the stitches unravelling and made into your own icon patches.

felting in a machine

Set the washing machine to, low water level, hot wash and cold rinse.

Add the piece of knitting, and some extra fabric (eg towel or old pair of jeans) to help create friction.

Add soap or detergent.

Run normal wash cycle.

Check to see if your knitting has felted. If you can still clearly see the stitches, repeat the washing.

felted butterfly

Measurements

Butterfly measures 15cm across

6"

Materials

Panda Woolbale 50 8 ply
(50g balls)

Main Colour	1
1st Contrast (C1)	1
2nd Contrast (C2)	1
3rd Contrast (C3)	1

Note: *Use only Panda Woolbale, as other yarns may not felt. One pair of 4.00mm (US 6) knitting needles or the required size to give correct tension; sewing needle and matching thread for joining butterfly.*

Tension

This butterfly has been designed at a tension of 22 sts and 30 rows to 10cm (4") over stocking st, using 4.00mm (US 6) needles.

Piece 1

Using 4.00mm (*US 6*) needles and MC, cast on 66 sts.
Work in stocking st until work measures 20cm (8") from beg.
Cast off.

Piece 2

Using 4.00mm (US 6) needles and C1, cast on 26 sts.
Work in stocking st until work measures 20cm (8") from beg.
Cast off.

Piece 3

Using 4.00mm (US 6) needles and C2, cast on 26 sts.
Work in stocking st until work measures 15cm (6") from beg.
Cast off.

Piece 4

Using 4.00mm (US 6) needles and C3, cast on 48 sts.
Work in stocking st until work measures 7cm (2") from beg.
Cast off.

Knitted Bobble (for head)

Using 4.00mm (US 6) needles and C3, cast on 10 sts.
Work 10 rows stocking st.
Cast off.
Gather edges into a ball and fill with scrap yarn before fastening securely.

To Make up

Felt all pieces and bobble thoroughly. Using template, cut 4 large wings from piece 1. Cut 2 small wings and 2 wing centres from piece 2. Cut 2 small wings from piece 3. Cut 2 wing centres and 1 body from piece 4. Sew tog as illustrated. Using 2 strands of C3, each 30cm (12") long, make a twisted cord (for antennae), knot each end and attach centre of cord to head.

felted flower

Measurements

Flower measures 14cm across	
	5"

Materials

Panda Woolbale 50 8 ply
(50g balls)

Main Colour	1
1st Contrast (C1)	1
2nd Contrast (C2)	1

Note: *Use only Panda Woolbale, as other yarns will not felt. One pair of 4.00mm (US 6) knitting needles or the required size to give correct tension; sewing needle and matching thread for joining flower.*

Tension

This flower has been designed at a tension of 22 sts and 30 rows to 10cm (4") over stocking st, using 4.00mm (US 6) needles.

Piece 1 (for petals)

Using 4.00mm (US 6) needles and MC, cast on 48 sts.
Work in stocking st until work measures 24cm (10") from beg.
Cast off.

Piece 2 (flower centre)

Using 4.00mm (US 6) needles and C1, cast on 22 sts.
Work in stocking st until work measures 13cm (5") from beg.
Cast off.

Knitted Bobble

Using 4.00mm (US 6) needles and C2, cast on 10 sts.
Work 10 rows stocking st.
Cast off.
Gather edges into a ball and fill with scrap yarn before fastening securely.

To make up

Felt both pieces and bobble thoroughly. Using template, cut 6 petals from piece 1 and flower centre from piece 2. Sew petals to back of flower centre and attach bobble to front of flower centre.

felted heart

Using 4.00mm (US 6) needles cast on 55 sts.
Work in stocking st until work measures 25cm (10") from beg.
Cast off.
Felt piece and cut out heart using template.

Heart for pompom scarf, legwarmers and heart beanie

Heart for large mittens

Heart for small mittens

templates for felting

Flower centre

Make 5

Flower petal (make 6)

Butterfly wings (make 4)

Butterfly wings

Butterfly body

First published in Australia in 2004
by Tracy Marsh Publications Pty Limited
ABN 98 008 122 405

PO Box 614 Unley SA 5061 Australia
Tel: (08) 8363 1248
Fax: (08) 8363 1352
Email: tracy@tracymarsh.com
www.tracymarsh.com for full range of
Tracy marsh Publications titles

Publisher: Tracy Marsh
Designer Illustrator: Tiffany Manuell
Graphic Designer: Kel Gibb
Photographer: Craig Arnold

The Publisher would like to thank
Australian Country Spinners for their
help with this publication.

National Library of Australia Cataloguing-in-Publication

data:

Marsh, Tracy, 1962-
Funky Knitting
ISBN 1 875899 21 9 (pbk)

1. Knitting. 2. Knitting – Patterns. 1 Manuell, Tiffany.
II. Title. (Series : Happy House craft series).

746.432

Produced by Phoenix Offset
Printed in Hong Kong